US–CUBA
RELATIONS

BY MICHAEL CAPEK

CONTENT CONSULTANT
RENATA KELLER
ASSISTANT PROFESSOR OF INTERNATIONAL RELATIONS
FREDERICK S. PARDEE SCHOOL OF GLOBAL STUDIES
BOSTON UNIVERSITY

Essential Library

An Imprint of Abdo Publishing | abdopublishing.com

abdopublishing.com

Published by Abdo Publishing, a division of ABDO, PO Box 398166, Minneapolis, Minnesota 55439. Copyright © 2016 by Abdo Consulting Group, Inc. International copyrights reserved in all countries. No part of this book may be reproduced in any form without written permission from the publisher. Essential Library™ is a trademark and logo of Abdo Publishing.

Printed in the United States of America, North Mankato, Minnesota
082015
012016

Cover Photo: Prensa Latina/Xinhua Press/Corbis
Interior Photos: Miguel Vinas/Prensa Latina/AP Images, 4–5; Raoul Fornezza/AP Images, 9; AP Images, 10–11, 14, 25, 26, 30–31; Red Line Editorial, 19; Andrew St. George/AP Images, 29; Cristoval Pascual/Prensa Latina/AP Images, 37; Carol M. Highsmith/Library of Congress, 40–41, 57; Alan Diaz/AP Images, 46–47; Bettmann/Corbis, 52–53; Stephan Savoia/AP Images, 58; Boris Yurchenko/AP Images, 62–63; Jose Goitia/AP Images, 66; Massimo Valicchia/NurPhoto/Sipa/AP Images, 69; Javier Galeano/AP Images, 70–71; Ramon Espinosa/AP Images, 77, 99; Brennan Linsley/AP Images, 78–79, 87; Mark Wilson/Pool/Reuters/Corbis, 83; Anna Jedynak/Shutterstock Images, 88–89; Mandel Ngan/AFP/Getty Images, 97

Editor: Mirella Miller
Series Designer: Maggie Villaume

Library of Congress Control Number: 2015944925

Cataloging-in-Publication Data

Capek, Michael.
 US-Cuba relations / Michael Capek.
  p. cm. -- (Special reports)
ISBN 978-1-62403-904-1 (lib. bdg.)
Includes bibliographical references and index.
1. United States--Foreign relations--Juvenile literature. 2. Cuba--Foreign relations--Juvenile literature. I. Title.
327.7307--dc23

                                                    2015944925

CONTENTS

CHAPTER ONE

A COLD WAR
SHOWDOWN

I n the darkness of April 16, 1961, a small fleet of ships moved into the Bay of Pigs, an inlet of the Gulf of Cazones on the southeastern coast of Cuba. Assault Brigade 2506 was made up of 1,500 trained fighters who were confident, armed, and ready for battle. Their mission was to storm ashore and begin a guerrilla war with one goal—to end Cuban president Fidel Castro's control of the government and his power over the people living on the small Caribbean island.

Although the fighters were mostly Cuban, agents of the US Central Intelligence Agency (CIA) organized the attack. The CIA recruited and trained the men, but US president John F. Kennedy ordered the CIA not to take part in any fighting. The mission was a Cuban rebellion.

Castro's supporters celebrate their victory after the Bay of Pigs invasion.

The United States had a replacement government ready to step in once Castro was eliminated. Castro's government was at odds with the United States, and the replacement government promised to be far friendlier.

REMOVING CASTRO

After President Fulgencio Batista fled Cuba in 1959, Castro's revolutionary government seized $1.8 billion of US money, property, and businesses in Cuba. Cuba was important to the United States because of its location and economy, but Castro was eager to prove he was in charge. According to the Inter-American Law Review, his actions resulted in the "largest uncompensated taking of American property by a foreign government in history."[1] Confiscating US properties and businesses were Castro's first steps toward turning Cuba into a socialist state. The Cuban government also began contacting leaders of the communist Soviet Union, the United States' most threatening enemy.

The United States, located only 90 miles (145 km) north of Cuba, could not tolerate the situation. As a member of the United Nations, however, the United States could not send its military power to invade Cuba. Such a move would appear to threaten other small Latin American nations and make the United States seem aggressive. A full military invasion would be costly in terms of lives lost and money spent. The United States had other weapons at its disposal, though. In November 1960, the US government imposed a trade embargo on Cuba. It forbade any US company or individual to do business with Cuba. The embargo was crippling for Cuba's economy. The United States had been Cuba's leading trade partner since the early 1900s.

THE COLD WAR

The term Cold War was used after World War II (1939–1945) to describe the political and military tension that developed between the United States and the Soviet Union. The United States and the Soviet Union were allies during the war, but afterward competition between their different political and economic ideas split them apart. The Soviet Union was guided by communism and socialism, while the United States followed democracy and capitalism. Communist and socialist nations usually are identified as those with a single-party, totalitarian government that owns and operates businesses and industries and controls land and money. Democratic nations generally are societies that allow the election of political leaders, free enterprise, accumulation of wealth, and private ownership of land and businesses.

THE BAY OF PIGS INVASION

The US government was secretly funding and supplying rebel groups inside Cuba. These groups were supposed to help Assault Brigade 2506 when they arrived at the Bay of Pigs. The invasion organizers expected thousands more Cubans, discontented with Castro, to join the revolt once they realized what was happening.

The invasion plan seemed foolproof, and the effort would result in Castro's removal from power and the birth of a new Cuban government. In the end, the Soviet threat would be eliminated, the trade embargo could be lifted, and the United States would emerge as the hero in the story. However, the Bay of Pigs invasion was a failure. Poor planning and timing doomed the invasion from the start. Castro learned of invasion preparations weeks in advance. He arrested thousands of Cubans he suspected of supporting the plot. Castro and his men spotted the assault brigade before they landed on April 16.

The invading rebels were met with intense resistance as they came ashore. Survivors took refuge in mosquito and snake-infested swamps, where they were later killed or captured. With no supporting rebel force to help them, Assault Brigade 2506 never got the chance to gain any ground. As a result, US ships and planes standing by to assist them could do little to help. There was no revolution

Castro's supporters were ready and waiting for the Bay of Pigs invasion on April 16.

to support. In less than three days, Castro's fighters killed 114 of the 1,500-man rebel assault brigade. They captured 1,179 men and seized huge numbers of weapons. Among the dead were several Americans. It was the evidence Castro needed to prove to the world the United States had led the invasion. Protests erupted in the United States and at some US embassies around the world. Even some of the United States' closest allies issued statements protesting the attacks.

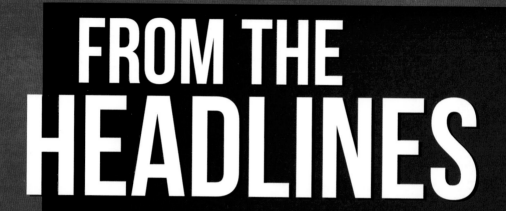

FROM THE HEADLINES

THE DAY THE BAY OF PIGS PRISONERS CAME HOME

After the invasion, Castro inspected the Assault Brigade 2506 prisoners. He recognized some as former Batista supporters who opposed or fought against him during the revolution. He had these people executed immediately. Castro paraded the other prisoners into Havana, Cuba's Sports Palace arena,

where he held televised "trials" for each of the prisoners. None of the men were allowed to speak in their own defense. Some of the prisoners were sentenced to years in Cuban prisons. Castro offered to return the rest of the prisoners to the United States in exchange for farm equipment or large sums of money from the US government. Former First Lady Eleanor Roosevelt and Milton Eisenhower, brother of the former president, offered to negotiate with Castro, but they could not work out a deal. Finally, after months of secret haggling, Castro agreed to accept a payment of $53 million in food and medicine, plus an extra $2.9 million in cash at the last minute, in exchange for 1,113 prisoners.[2]

On December 29, 1962, President Kennedy and First Lady Jacqueline Kennedy welcomed home the prisoners in a ceremony at Miami's Orange Bowl. The brigade presented the president with their flag. Kennedy told them, "I assure you this flag will be returned to this brigade in a free Havana."[3] That did not happen. Kennedy was assassinated one year later, and Castro stayed in power.

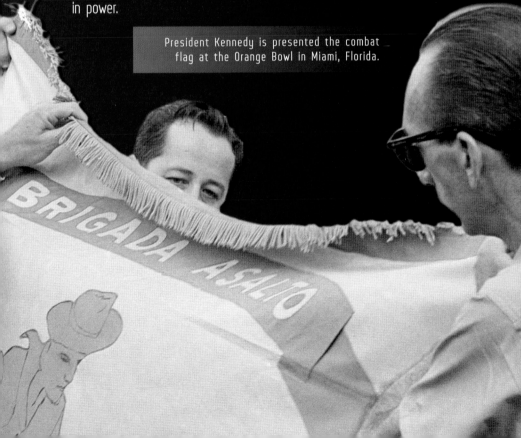

President Kennedy is presented the combat flag at the Orange Bowl in Miami, Florida.

THE MISSILES OF OCTOBER

The failed Bay of Pigs invasion strengthened Castro's image in Cuba and around the world. But he knew the United States would not stop trying to remove him from power. Castro was more determined than ever to prove to the United States Cuba would not be bullied. In December 1961, Castro announced he intended to seek the aid of the Soviet Union, making Cuba a strong socialist state. He invited Soviet officials to Cuba and asked for military and economic help.

Soviets moved swiftly in 1961 and 1962 to sign new trade agreements that boosted Cuba's economy. At the same time, the Soviets hurried planes, weapons, military trainers, and advisers to Cuba. The opportunity to get a foothold

OPERATION MONGOOSE

After the Bay of Pigs invasion, the United States set in motion an elaborate plan to weaken Castro's image in Cuba and remove him from power. Operation Mongoose began in November 1961. CIA agents took part in secret, undercover activities, such as assisting and supplying anti-Castro groups in Cuba. Activities also included direct attempts to kill Castro. Creative plot ideas involved poisoning Castro's cigars, rigging a seashell with explosives and laying it on his favorite beach, and placing disease germs in his scuba gear. Operation Mongoose was as much a fiasco as the Bay of Pigs invasion. The failed activities only made the CIA look bad and convinced Castro the United States was against him.

close to the United States and test the US president's nerve was too good to pass up.

Following the political and diplomatic disaster that occurred at the Bay of Pigs, the United States drew a firestorm of criticism from around the world, particularly from the Soviet Union. A little more than a year after the battle, the US government announced plans to take further actions against Cuba. On the evening of October 22, 1962, President Kennedy appeared on television with news that shocked the world. He had photographs from a US spy plane that clearly showed nuclear missile launching sites under construction in Cuba. The Soviet-supplied weapons, he explained, would be able to fire missiles armed with nuclear bombs at targets in North and South America.

Few people needed to be told what this meant. Horrific images of nuclear devastation and suffering inflicted on Japan at the end of World War II were burned into everyone's consciousness. The thought that two of the United States' most dangerous enemies, the Soviet Union and Cuba, had nuclear weapons pointed toward the country was terrifying. Even worse was the realization the United States had nuclear weapons just as powerful pointing back.

President Kennedy did not sugarcoat the crisis or the actions required to end it. He made it clear the United States would not tolerate this sort of aggression. The missiles and launchers needed to be removed immediately, and no more nuclear weapons could be delivered to the island. To make this happen, Kennedy explained he was imposing a naval quarantine on Cuba. A virtual wall of ships would encircle the island and block Soviet ships from getting through.

A crucial moment came on October 24, as Soviet ships bound for Cuba approached the line of US ships.

US antiaircraft missiles sit ready for launch in Key West, Florida, in 1962.

If the Soviets had tried to break through the blockade, US ships would have moved to stop them. If anyone on either side had fired, a military confrontation could have escalated into a nuclear war. At the last moment, the Soviet ships stopped and turned around. A few days later, Cuba shot down a US plane. A US invasion force waiting in Florida was put on alert. "I thought it was the last Saturday I would ever see," US Secretary of Defense Robert McNamara said later.[4] President Kennedy decided not to order an attack. Instead, he accelerated talks with Soviet leader Nikita Khrushchev.

On November 20, Kennedy announced a formal end to the Cuban Missile Crisis. Soviet leaders agreed to remove nuclear weapons from Cuba. In exchange, the United

THE MEANING OF THE MISSILE CRISIS

As one writer has said, Cuba's "relations with the United States are still held hostage to the missile crisis."[5] In other words, the issues that grew out of that event are still not resolved. Cuba was outraged by the Soviet handling of the Cuban Missile Crisis, convinced the Soviets backed down and removed the missiles much too quickly. Castro wanted to take a much tougher stand. He had hoped Cuba and the Soviet Union would stand together and force the United States to back down. Then, together, they could begin spreading the socialist revolution around the world. When the Soviets gave in without consulting Castro, he felt betrayed. He would never again fully trust the ability of Soviet leadership to make important decisions about Cuba's future or its role in world politics.

States secretly agreed to dismantle their missile bases in Turkey, near the Soviet Union. They also agreed never again to invade Cuba.

NOW AND THEN

US relations with Cuba are very different today, almost the exact opposite of what they were in 1962. Castro is no longer the powerful leader he once was. Advancing age and poor health removed him from the world stage. In the 2000s, his brother Raúl—who is also old—began acting as Cuba's principal leader. It is believed other trusted advisers are playing an increasingly important role in steering Cuba toward a future without a Castro in a position of power.

The future of US-Cuba relations is unknown, but there are many reasons for optimism. In 2015, for the first time in more than 50 years, the US and Cuban presidents sat together and talked, agreeing the two

"IN CUBA WE WERE GOING TO CONSTRUCT SOCIALISM IN THE MOST ORDERLY POSSIBLE MANNER, WITHIN A REASONABLE AMOUNT OF TIME, WITH THE LEAST AMOUNT OF TRAUMA OR PROBLEMS, BUT THE AGGRESSIONS OF IMPERIALISM ACCELERATED THE REVOLUTIONARY PROCESS."[6]

—FIDEL CASTRO, DESCRIBING HOW HOSTILE ACTIONS OF THE UNITED STATES HELPED ENSURE CUBA'S FUTURE AS A COMMUNIST STATE

nations should reestablish diplomatic relations. President Barack Obama said it was time to end the crippling trade embargo imposed on Cuba. Raúl said Cubans are eager to discuss the embargo and the many other issues that still divide the United States and Cuba. Some restrictions, such as travel, have been eased, clearing the way for more positive changes. There are many more obstacles to face, however. Many Cuban Americans, for example, believe the Cuban government needs to change the way it treats Cubans. Also, the US Congress must decide whether to remove the trade embargo.

Certainly, the trade embargo, the Bay of Pigs invasion, and the Cuban Missile Crisis did not cause the tension that existed for more than five decades between the United States and Cuba. They were merely a turning point in the long and troubled relationship between the neighboring nations. The ongoing debate over issues that still divide and connect people today—immigration, free trade, national security, and human rights—began long before the 1960s. To fully understand today's issues, it is necessary to examine how the conflict between the United States and Cuba developed.

CHAPTER TWO

UNEASY NEIGHBORS

E ven in the country's early days, the United States' Founding Fathers believed Cuba might someday become a US possession. The island's prime location, guarding the entrance to the Caribbean Sea and Gulf of Mexico, made it significant militarily and economically. In the years before the American Civil War (1861–1865), US slaveholders urged the government to buy or seize the island from Spain, which had ruled Cuba for 400 years. With abolitionists opposing the spread of slavery in the rapidly growing United States, slave owners and traders looked longingly at Cuba's tropical climate and slave-driven economy. The American Civil War settled the issue, however. The US slave plantation system was destroyed, and Spain held

Early US leaders assumed Cuba would come under US control sooner or later, simply because it was so close geographically.

on to the island throughout the 1800s.

During the 1800s, Cubans embraced the idea of independence from Spain, and some favored annexation by the United States as the best way to accomplish that end. A US military takeover of the island sounded appealing to the United States too, but leaders in Washington, DC, had no desire for a war with Spain.

From the 1860s to 1890s, a greater sense of Cuban national identity and pride developed into an open rebellion against Spanish political and military control. Cuban rebels repeatedly declared their independence from Spain and battled with Spanish forces during the Ten Years' War (1868–1878) and again from 1895 to 1898.

GOING TO WAR

US President William McKinley felt intense pressure to send troops to Cuba but feared a war with Spain would be costly. The issue was decided for him on the morning of

February 15, 1898, when the US battleship *Maine* suddenly exploded in Havana's harbor, killing 258 US sailors. Although Spain denied responsibility for the sinking, US reaction was swift and intense. President McKinley sent a declaration of war to Congress on April 11, 1898.

The Spanish-American War was the shortest war in US history, lasting just four months. Spain surrendered in August 1898 after its naval fleet was destroyed, which left the United States in control of Cuba and several other overseas territories. As President McKinley had feared, it cost more than 2,000 Americans their lives. In the aftermath, the United States found itself in military control of an island whose people were discontented and wanted independence.

JOSÉ MARTÍ

One of the most important Cuban rebel leaders in exile during the 1800s was José Martí. A poet, inspirational speaker, and political activist, Martí was imprisoned at age 16 by Spanish authorities for plotting against them. He spent the rest of his life speaking, writing, and fighting for Cuba's rebellion against foreign influences. While living in the United States, Martí worked tirelessly for Cuban independence. But he did not live to see his dream come true. He returned to Cuba in 1895 and was killed fighting against the Spanish soon after. His writing and actions inspired millions of Cubans and people from other Caribbean islands to continue to struggle for independence. In his final letter before his death, Martí urged Cubans to do everything they could to prevent "the USA from spreading over the West Indies and falling . . . upon other lands of Our America."[2]

MORE TO THE
STORY

ROOSEVELT TO THE RESCUE

Assistant Secretary of the Navy Theodore Roosevelt ensured the United States had a modern, fully equipped naval fleet in the spring of 1898. Influenced by the ideas of US Navy Admiral Alfred Thayer Mahan, Roosevelt believed the great nations in history always had the most powerful navies. He pushed and prodded Secretary of the Navy John Long to modernize and add to the United States' fleet of warships. Long was opposed to war, but Roosevelt thought the US should take a more active role in shaping world affairs. In fact, he desperately wanted a war with Spain.

When the Spanish-American War started, Roosevelt and Army Colonel Leonard Wood recruited and trained volunteers, forming the First United States Volunteer Cavalry, or what became known as the Rough Riders. The unit fought in several small battles in Cuba, though none impacted the overall outcome of the war. Still, news stories describing Roosevelt leading charges at Santiago and San Juan Hill made him famous. So did Roosevelt's own written accounts of his adventures and reenactments filmed long after the war was over. Roosevelt's cowboy antics during the Spanish-American War helped put him in a position to assume the presidency when William McKinley was assassinated in 1901. His hard-charging personality and daring deeds symbolized the approach he and most other US leaders took whenever they dealt with Cuba.

YANKEE GO HOME

The United States offered Cubans their independence in 1903, after Cuba was forced to accept the terms of the Platt Amendment. This addition to the Cuban constitution was a landmark in US foreign policy and established rigid conditions that would guide US-Cuba relations for years to come. The basis of this rigid law was a widely accepted idea that Cubans were a weak and inferior people who needed a strong hand to guide them. As US President William Howard Taft said, the United States wanted to make an "earnest effort to uplift these people, to help them on their way to self-government, and to teach them a higher and better civilization."[3] This principle became the backbone of US policy for years. The Platt Amendment gave the United States both the right and the responsibility to oversee all happenings in Cuba. The United States could install leaders who were more attentive to US interests than those of the Cuban people.

The United States' superior attitude persisted throughout the 1930s, as riots, protests, and cries from Cubans for more sovereignty grew increasingly insistent.

A series of US ambassadors and political advisers in Havana tried to maneuver affairs and events and bring order to the island. Several military interventions to protect US interests or control minor revolts only made matters worse. "Yankee go home" became a commonly heard shout and a frequently seen slogan on signs in towns and villages across Cuba.

UPHEAVAL AND NEW POWER

In 1934, as part of the Good Neighbor policy toward Latin-American countries, President Franklin D. Roosevelt repealed the treaty that enforced the Platt Amendment. His actions stopped direct US military interventions, but it did not end the United States' constant oversight of Cuban affairs or the peoples' growing discontent. The United States still sought to uplift and guide Cubans. As a result, social and political upheavals continued to rock the island throughout the 1940s. Over the years, various US presidents, as well as agents in Havana, continued blaming Cuba's leaders for being too weak or corrupt to govern properly. Mostly, they blamed the unrest on the unwillingness of the Cuban people to accept a US-style government rather than listening to the promises of communists. After World War II, Cold War tension with the Soviet Union and Soviet attempts to gain control elsewhere in the world in the 1950s worried the US government more than any other situation.

In 1952, the United States backed Cuban dictator Fulgencio Batista. Batista promised to establish a more democratic government, allow more US business investment, and stop communist influences in Cuba. He made good on most of his promises but used brutal, repressive methods to do so. Under his rule, while US

Cubans wave banners and flags in protest of the Platt Amendment as they walk through the streets of Havana.

Under Batista, Cuba appeared a peaceful and happy paradise to tourists and outsiders traveling there. But it was an illusion.

officials looked the other way, Cuba became a police state.

People were routinely murdered, threatened, and denied

due process in courts. They also were denied the ability

to speak freely. Batista's gangs attacked anyone who

spoke against him. Thousands of Cubans fled the country.

Simmering just beneath the surface was long-standing

discontentment among Cuba's people, particularly the

poor and middle classes. For years, a revolutionary spirit

had been forming. All it needed was the right situation

and the right person to bring it into the open.

THE JULY 26 MOVEMENT

The first rumblings of the Cuban Revolution came in the

early morning hours of July 26, 1953. On that day, a group

of 100 guerrilla fighters attacked the Moncada Barracks, an army fortress and barracks near the town of Santiago, Cuba. Fidel Castro, a 26-year-old lawyer and politician, and his younger brother, Raúl, led the raid. Their goal was lofty: to free Cuba from the terrorist rule of Batista.

The Moncada raid was a total failure. Seventy of the rebels were caught and killed by Batista's forces.[4] Fidel and Raúl were arrested and imprisoned for less than two years. Upon their release, however, they continued plotting the overthrow of Batista. Their efforts became known as the July 26 Movement after the date of their attack on the Moncada Barracks.

During their exile, Fidel and Raúl trained another army of rebels and led them back to Cuba in December 1956, this time to stage a major revolution. For two years, from secluded mountain hideouts, the brothers' band of guerrilla fighters fought Batista's larger and better-armed military force to a standstill. With each victory, the revolutionary July 26 Movement gained popularity and support throughout Cuba. Raúl's gift for military strategy and Fidel's personal charm attracted and persuaded people of all classes and types to join them and the cause for Cuban freedom.

Supporters staged acts of sabotage and resistance against the government. They produced a flood of propaganda and wrote articles in magazines and newspapers about the revolution. Stories in the US media made the movement's leaders popular heroes in the United States, as well as in Cuba. Bearded and smiling Fidel, with machine gun in one hand and cigar in the other, became the face of the revolution. As his fame increased, so did the number of Cubans who supported the movement and turned away from Batista.

By 1958, the US government, which had originally supported Batista, turned against him as well. The flow of weapons and money from the United States stopped. As Batista's military power waned, Fidel's rebels continued advancing. Batista fled Cuba

"THE PROBLEM IS, OF COURSE, THAT MOST PEOPLE DO NOT WANT A NEIGHBORING POWER TO LIFT THEM UP, REGARDLESS OF HOW WELL INTENTIONED THE EFFORT MIGHT BE, AND CUBA'S REVOLUTIONARY GENERATION GREW UP IN A SOCIETY THAT LEFT IT PARTICULARLY OPPOSED TO UPLIFTING BY THE UNITED STATES."[5]

—LARS SCHOULTZ, AUTHOR, HISTORIAN, AND PAST PRESIDENT OF THE LATIN AMERICAN STUDIES ASSOCIATION

Raúl, *left*, and Fidel, *center*, and their rebel fighters succeeded in taking control of the government in 1959.

on January 1, 1959, handing control over to Fidel and his revolutionary movement.

In 1959, Fidel officially entered Havana and began the process of consolidating control. He set up a government, with himself as military commander in chief and named Raúl defense minister. If anything happened to Fidel, Raúl would take over and continue leading the revolution.

CHAPTER THREE

FIDEL CASTRO'S
SUPPORTERS

Castro's actions following his takeover in 1959 were anything but democratic. He violently seized power, established a single-party system of government with himself as the supreme leader, and denied basic freedoms to his people for more than 50 years. Yet Castro still has many admirers and defenders. Presidents before him used terror, extreme violence, corruption, and gang warfare. Castro's rise to power ended these actions. He stood up for the poor and helpless and installed a socialist society based on equality and fairness. His defenders argue that if he has been harsh at times, it is because he had to be. Attacked by the United States from all sides, he was forced to rule with toughness.

Many Castro defenders point out no other leader was able to stabilize Cuba the way Castro did.

Those who defend Castro say he never threatened the United States unless the US government or its agents first threatened him or Cuba. Castro's defenders point to studies and reports by independent scholars and investigators as proof. One expert said the entire US intelligence community agrees Castro "poses no significant security threat to the United States."[1] In fact, in April 2015, President Obama announced the removal of Cuba from the US list of state sponsors of terrorism.

Many of Castro's improvements made Cuba a better place to live. His establishment of a Ministry of Social Welfare, for instance, instituted free health-care programs and free food and medicine for the poor and elderly. His Ministry of Housing dramatically reduced the price of houses and apartments and

CUBA AND TERRORISM

Cuba was on the United States' list of nations who support or sponsor terrorism for more than 30 years. Some of the reasons Cuba was on the list were the nation's close relationship with North Korea and Castro's support of Central-American revolutionary movements in the 1980s. Another reason was because Cuba provides sanctuary for people the United States sees as terrorist threats. One of the most controversial people is Joanne Chesimard. She is a member of the Black Liberation Army who killed a New Jersey police officer in 1973. She escaped to Cuba, where she has remained ever since. She was named to the Most Wanted Terrorists list by the Federal Bureau of Investigation (FBI), which has offered a $2 million reward for her return.[2]

made it illegal for landlords to evict tenants. His literacy programs educated millions, and his organization of microbrigades, or teams of volunteer civilian workers, built homes for those who could not otherwise afford them. Cuba's general standard of living improved dramatically during Castro's early years in power.

CASTRO'S CRITICS

Most observers of the Castro regime, however, are less willing to overlook Castro's faults. After he seized power, Castro organized Cuba's government and society so he made all decisions solely. His word was law, even if he changed his mind from day to day or year to year.

CASTRO'S LITERACY CAMPAIGN OF 1961

Perhaps one of Castro's greatest successes was his 1961 campaign to eliminate illiteracy. In 1959, when Castro took power, 40 percent of Cuba's population could not read or write. In 1960, in a speech at the United Nations, Castro made a promise he would eliminate illiteracy in Cuba within one year. To accomplish this goal, he recruited and trained 100,000 student teachers and sent them into the countryside, where most illiterate people lived. Alone, armed only with books and an oil lamp, these idealistic young people, most of them teenage girls, traveled to remote parts of the island to teach young and old people to read. It was sometimes dangerous. More than 40 student teachers were killed. Yet, within one year, these teachers succeeded in teaching more than 1 million Cubans to read and write. Castro quickly built schools across Cuba where none had been before. Hundreds of thousands of Cuban children went to school for the first time.[3]

Accusations of human rights abuses have followed the Cuban government since its beginning. Castro and his revolutionaries arrested many supporters of the former Batista government and armed forces. The United States strongly criticized the trials that followed, which largely ignored standard legal procedures and practices. The United States and others also criticized the severity of sentences, ranging from long prison terms to immediate execution. The Cuban military, organized and run by Raúl, has always supported Fidel with unswerving loyalty.

Castro did not need violent soldiers to repress his people. He was extremely skilled at using social pressure and patriotic appeals to get the population to do what he wanted. He knew how to use his own personal charm and charisma, as well. When it became clear people were speaking or acting against him, Castro quickly locked up or exiled people. He did this in 1999 with criminals and traitors. It was one of the most severe lockups in decades. The number of political prisoners in Cuban prisons is not known, but it is thought to be in the thousands.

Castro's dictatorial, oppressive behavior is one important reason the United States and other nations have

MORE TO THE
STORY

FIDEL'S POWER OF WORDS

Similar to many leaders in history, Castro knew how to use the power of his words and voice to move and inspire people. Many people trace much of Castro's success to this ability. He discovered his gift for public speaking and honed it during his education and training as a lawyer.

Observers have described Castro as a master at using his voice, body language, and facial expressions. He has the ability to change volume, emphasize certain words and ideas, insert meaningful pauses, and use gestures and facial expressions to keep audiences attentive even during long speeches. Many of Castro's speeches were very long.

It was Castro's passion for long speeches that revealed his ill health. In June 2001, Castro fainted as he stood to deliver a speech in Havana's blazing sun. It was the first time many Cubans saw the frailty and advancing age of their leader.

opposed Castro all these years. Critics say Castro's whims and obsessions have harmed Cuba and imposed hardship and suffering on his people. Even one of Castro's former supporters, Juan Antonio Rodriguez Menier, a former official from the Cuban Ministry of the Interior, said, "Fidel has manipulated the poverty of his once relatively well-off country in order to maintain his personal power and pursue his private agenda."[4]

RISE UP AND REVOLT

A poll conducted in 1981 found 71 percent of Cubans considered themselves "enemies of Fidel Castro's government." In 1993, a former high-level official in Cuba estimated only 10 percent of Cubans sympathized with Castro.[5] This raises the question: Why have Cubans never revolted against their leaders?

The fact is, while many Cubans are frustrated with the Castros' political and economic failures, they admire the brothers for their revolutionary principles and for standing up to the United States. Among other reasons, Cubans value family above almost everything, and respect for one's elders is important. One historian described

The Castro brothers are similar to beloved national grandfathers, as well as elder statesmen.

Fidel as being "like an aging rock star" to Cuba's younger generation.[6]

Fear of government retaliation is one major reason Cubans do not revolt. Every Cuban child studies the Escambray Rebellion, or what Castro calls the War Against the Bandits. Batista followers and rural farmers in the Escambray Mountains undertook this six-year uprising in the 1960s. They resisted the Soviet-style communist programs advocated by Castro's regime. Castro sent thousands of troops to face off against the rebels, many of whom were executed.

Vocal opponents of Castro's government appear from time to time. Other groups that dare to stage or support rebellions have met much the same fate as the Escambray Rebellion fighters. Protesters and demonstrators against Castro are often arrested, and there has never been any significant sign of a single leader attempting to seize power from the current government, as the Castros did in 1959. This is partly due to peoples' fear that the government's military and legal system are more than capable of crushing any show of opposition.

Perhaps the main reason Cubans are content to wait until Castro's government comes to a natural end is because the Castro brothers are old and ill. In July 2006, Fidel, at age 81 and in poor health after surgery, temporarily handed over power to 76-year-old Raúl and several trusted cabinet

CHE GUEVARA

While in exile in Mexico, Castro met Ernesto Che Guevara, a young doctor and passionate revolutionary from Argentina. Guevara and Castro formed an immediate bond based on their socialist ideals and shared hatred of the United States. Guevara vowed allegiance to the revolutionary cause and swore to support Castro in liberating the Cuban people. Few people influenced Castro as much as Guevara. His ideas, particularly on economy and spreading the revolution globally, were the basis for much of Castro's thoughts and actions. When Guevara was killed fighting with rebels in Bolivia in 1967, Castro declared three days of official mourning in Cuba.

ministers. The exchange of power became permanent in February 2008, and Fidel rarely has appeared in public since. False rumors he is dead have circulated for years.

"WHEN THIS WAR IS OVER A MUCH WIDER AND BIGGER WAR WILL COMMENCE FOR ME: THE WAR I AM GOING TO WAGE AGAINST [THE UNITED STATES]. I AM AWARE THAT THIS IS MY TRUE DESTINY."[7]

—FIDEL CASTRO, REFERRING TO THE ESCAMBRAY REBELLION IN A 1958 LETTER TO A FRIEND

TRAVELING TO AND FROM CUBA

Two nations only 90 miles (145 km) apart, especially ones sharing a long history and a water border, cannot remain forever isolated from one another. Issues and events constantly push and pull the United States and Cuba together, reluctant though they may be to communicate. The United States protects a sizeable number of Cubans who for one reason or another fled their island home and settled in the United States. The official US census in 2010 recorded the presence of nearly 1.8 million Cuban Americans

Festivals and holidays in the Little Havana neighborhood of Miami, Florida, feature Cuban food, music, and art.

on US soil.[1] In 2015, the number is estimated at closer to 2.1 million.[2]

The migration of people from Cuba to the United States began almost as soon as Castro took power. The first people to leave the country were former supporters of the Batista government. More than 40,000 Cubans left in the first two years of the Castro regime.[3] Beginning in 1960 and lasting until 1962, Operation Pedro Pan occurred, one of the largest emigrations in Cuba's history. The Catholic Welfare Bureau in the United States organized this mass evacuation. The airlift moved more than 14,000 children.[4] They were sent to the United States by Cuban parents who were worried about how the new government would treat children.

LITTLE HAVANA

Of the Cubans who live in the United States, approximately 1.2 million live in Miami, Florida.[5] One part of the city is known locally as Little Havana. The Cuban community is proud of its unique culture and heritage and seeks ways to celebrate it. Locals honor their heritage by continuing to oppose the Castro brothers, whom they blame for their departure from Cuba. One way they do this is by organizing and supporting programs that assist others wishing to flee Cuba. They also work with groups, such as the Cuban American National Foundation, and as individuals to make sure important issues are kept alive in the public debate. Many Cuban Americans support political candidates they believe share their special interests and concerns and oppose those who do not.

During the missile crisis of 1962 and for three years thereafter, legal emigrations from Cuba stopped entirely. However, many people still tried to leave illegally. Hundreds of Cubans set off in boats of all sizes, an incredibly risky venture in waters famous for storms that sweep in from the Atlantic Ocean without warning.

On September 29, 1965, Castro announced a new policy stating people were free to leave Cuba. There would be no more flights to the United States, but people who wished to emigrate could gather at the Cuban port of Camarioca. Boats from the United States could come and pick them up. Thousands of people massed at the port, and hundreds of boats from Florida arrived to get them. The boats often were in poor condition, piloted by people with little ocean experience. Several boats sank, and dozens of people drowned before Castro stopped the boatlift in November 1965. Approximately 3,000 Cubans left the country between October and November.[6]

Beginning in November 1965, Castro and US President Lyndon B. Johnson agreed to allow evacuation flights from Cuba to begin again. These flights continued for six years and cost the US government $50 million.[7] By the end of the 1980s, nearly 1 million Cubans had moved to the United States.[8] That was nearly 10 percent of the entire Cuban population.[9] President Johnson signed the Cuban Adjustment Act in 1966, which gave temporary parole status to any Cuban refugee who landed in the United States. One year later, they were given permanent legal residency. This caused many Cubans to again set sail in unseaworthy crafts.

WET FOOT, DRY FOOT

Changes in the Cuban Adjustment Act in the mid-1990s were known as the "wet-foot, dry-foot policy."[11] According to the policy, Cubans who arrived on land—or dry foot—at any US border could enter the country. But if they were caught at sea—or wet foot— they would be sent back to Cuba. Smugglers bringing people from Cuba to the United States started using high-powered speedboats to outrun the coast guards of both countries. They charged huge sums of money to deliver Cubans to Florida beaches.

Another massive boatlift occurred in the autumn of 1980, under President Jimmy Carter. At the end of the Mariel Boatlift, approximately 250,000 Cubans moved to the United States.[10]

Thousands of Cubans still come to the United States each year. In 2014, approximately 30,000 Cubans fled to the United States via the Straits of Florida or by air. Reports show some migrants try to leave Cuba five to ten times before they successfully make it to the United States.

MORE TO THE
STORY

THE MARIEL BOATLIFT

Cuban Americans have influenced politics in Cuba and had an impact on Fidel Castro. One example is from 1980, during the Jimmy Carter administration. President Carter contacted Castro, who agreed to allow Cuban Americans to return to Cuba on a limited basis so they could visit relatives. The agreement resulted in many reunions, as Cubans met with family they had not seen or spoken to in decades. However, upon realizing their relatives were living in much better conditions in the United States, many Cubans wanted to better their own situation. In 1980, riots and demonstrations began in Havana, prompting demands for Castro to allow another emigration to the United States, as he had done in the 1960s. Finally, Castro agreed, but he was angry at the United States and the Cuban Americans who had stirred up anger. Castro announced the United States could send boats to the Cuban port of Mariel to pick up Cubans who wished to emigrate. He then emptied prisons and mental hospitals, rounded up troublemakers and criminals, and sent them to Mariel as well.

FROM THE
HEADLINES

ELIÁN GONZALEZ

Early Thanksgiving Day morning in 1999, a fisherman rescued a five-year-old boy floating in an inner tube in the Gulf of Mexico. The boy was Elián Gonzalez. He and his mother had been trying to escape to the United States when their boat sank. Elián's mother and ten others died. The arrival of Elián Gonzalez in the United States set off a debate and a series of events that gained worldwide attention for the next five months. Relatives of Elián's mother took him in as soon as the boy arrived on US soil. But Elián had other relatives in Miami and a father and grandparents in Cuba who wanted custody. A court battle followed, with the governments of both nations making demands and offering support to various sides. Castro made anti-American speeches and organized huge public demonstrations. The Cuban-American community also demonstrated, insisting Elián be protected from the Castro regime. In the end, the courts ruled in favor of Elián's father. Welcomed back to Cuba by Castro and cheering crowds, Elián was treated as a national hero before he returned to a quieter life.

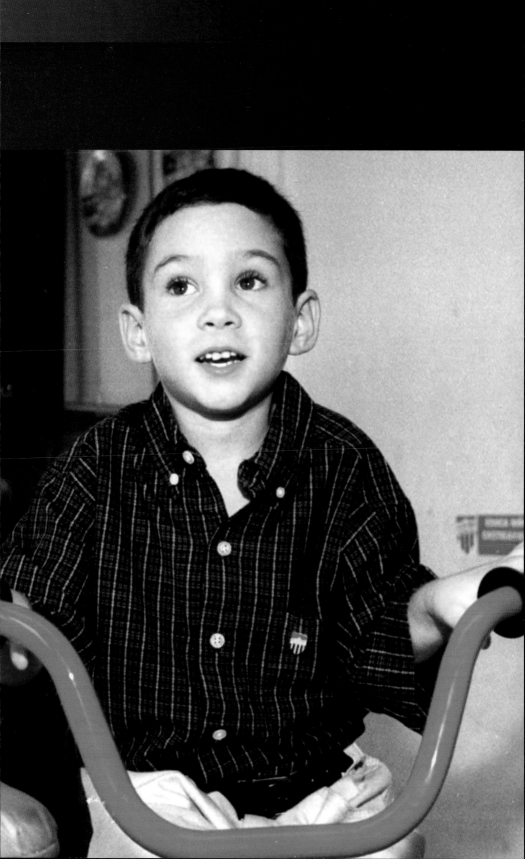

But studies do not show how many people have tried and died attempting to make the dangerous journey over the past 50 years. One writer even called the Straits of Florida "one of the world's largest aquatic graveyards."[12]

OPENING THE DOOR

American tourists are not generally permitted to travel to Cuba, except under specific conditions. Cuban Americans, however, have been allowed to travel to and from Cuba for years. At one point, the US government restricted the amount of time they could stay and the amount of money they could spend while in Cuba, but those restrictions eased over the years. The situation changed in 2004, when a US government report stated approximately 125,000 Cuban Americans traveled to Cuba each year.[13] The report claimed many of those returning were people who took huge amounts of money and unlimited quantities of goods and clothing to their Cuban relatives. It was clear billions of dollars were pouring into the Cuban economy each year. Alarmed, the US Congress made immediate changes to travel regulations. Only Cuban Americans who had close relatives back home could travel to Cuba, and they were allowed only one trip every three years, as opposed to one per year. Visits could last no more than 14 days, and visitors could spend no more than $50 per day and could carry only $300 total. Finally, visitors were permitted to bring only 44 pounds (20 kg) of luggage. Castro called these changes cruel.[14]

Most of the restrictions stayed in place until 2009, when the Obama administration began making changes. These changes included allowing US citizens to travel to Cuba with certain restrictions. Most trips were allowed under what were called "people-to-people" programs, established to allow Cubans and Americans to interact for the first time in decades. On January 20, 2015, the US government relaxed restrictions even further, making it easier for Americans to travel to Cuba. Most people still need a specific reason to travel to Cuba, such as

BROTHERS TO THE RESCUE

In 1996, the US government ordered the group Brothers to the Rescue to stop assisting Cubans trying to escape the island nation. The Cuban-American group had six small planes that flew over the gulf between Cuba and the United States. They searched for Cubans in boats and sent rescue boats to help them. Brothers to the Rescue ignored the US order, as well as one from Fidel ordering them not to enter Cuban airspace. In February 1996, the Cuban Air Force shot down two of the planes that strayed too close to Cuba. The incident caused uproar in the Cuban-American community.

professional research, educational activities, or programs in support of the Cuban people. Previously, Americans had to apply for a travel license to partake in such activities, but that step is no longer necessary. However, the new regulations still ban visits solely for tourism.

TRADING WITH THE ENEMY

The tension between the United States and Cuba has never been about contact between the citizens of each country. One issue has always been money. The Trading with the Enemy Act of 1963 made it a crime for US citizens to spend money in Cuba. The act was designed to keep US dollars from aiding Castro's government. US citizens other than Cuban Americans have found ways to travel to Cuba over the years, and the US government has, from time to time, fined them $250,000 or ten years in prison.[15]

Most Americans want sanctions removed, which directly opposes the wishes of some Cuban Americans. Representatives from areas where large numbers of Cuban Americans live, such as southern Florida, exert tremendous pressure in Washington, DC. It is largely because of them that presidents over the years have been reluctant to end travel and other sanctions against Cuba. Many younger Cubans see progress and believe relations between the United States and Cuba must improve. A large number of Cubans have relatives in the United States, making it difficult to justify keeping the two nations apart.

"WHILE MANY CUBANS WILL WANT TO LEAVE CUBA, FEW CUBAN-AMERICANS WOULD ABANDON THEIR LIFE IN THE UNITED STATES AND RETURN TO THE ISLAND, ESPECIALLY IF CUBA EXPERIENCES A SLOW TRANSITION PERIOD [AFTER THE CASTROS ARE GONE]."[16]

—JAIME SUCHLICKI, CUBAN SCHOLAR AND HISTORIAN, 2002

CHAPTER FIVE

THE EMBARGO DEBATE

The US embargo against Cuba is one of the longest in history and the largest obstacle in normalizing relations between the two nations. Generally, an embargo is a type of sanction. It is an economic tool used by one nation to show its displeasure with another nation by stopping trade between them. An embargo is a tactic nations use to avoid direct military action, such as invasion or bombing.

The Cuba embargo began as an arms embargo in 1958. It stopped the sale of US weapons to Cuba during Castro's fight with Batista. But in November 1960, President Dwight D. Eisenhower extended the embargo to include all goods except food and medicine. The

In 1962, President Kennedy signed an arms embargo against Cuba.

reasons for Eisenhower's extreme action were Castro's seizing and nationalizing of US properties in Cuba, as well as his establishment of relations with the Soviet Union. Eisenhower severed all diplomatic relations with Cuba in January 1961.

The US government has, from time to time, objected strongly to Castro's foreign military efforts. For example, Castro supported and encouraged revolutions in other parts of the world, particularly in Africa and Latin America between the 1960s and 1980s.

Most of the grievances against Castro come under the heading of human rights violations—continuing to deny Cuban citizens basic rights—mainly free speech, travel, elections, and public assembly. Seizing and holding political prisoners and generally mistreating those in custody are also on the list.

From the 1990s into the 2000s, the United States most often said the embargo was still in place "to seek a peaceful transition to democracy and a resumption of economic growth in Cuba."[1] In other words, the United States hoped strong sanctions would cause enough economic hardship for Cuba that Castro would give up power or the Cuban people would rise up and take it from him. Then, a new, democratic, more US-friendly government could take control of Cuba.

KEEPING THE EMBARGO

The debate whether the embargo is right or wrong has raged on for years. Those in favor of keeping the embargo argue Castro's dictatorship denies people's fundamental liberty and basic human rights. Secondly, they argue the only way to change Castro's dictatorship is to put him under political and economic pressure. Critics point out it is not the embargo but rather Castro's failed ideas and repression that created the poor conditions in Cuba. Despite the embargo, the United States continues to send food and medicine to the island nation and allows doctors and humanitarian workers to aid the needy in Cuba.

GOING TO EXTREMES

The United States has, at times, gone to extremes interpreting the embargo. In the mid-1960s, and again in the 1980s, stainless steel cookware became hard to find in US stores. The shortages resulted from decisions by Presidents Johnson and Ronald Reagan to limit the import of any product containing nickel mined in Cuba. Also during the Reagan administration, the government began banning books and magazines imported from Cuba. A ban on importing any kind of Cuban artwork remained in effect until 1991.

Some US citizens are in favor of the embargo because they believe Cuba is a continuing threat to the United States' war on terror. Castro said in the past he would do anything to attack the United States. As such, it is possible he would harbor terrorists and give them a place from which to launch attacks. As well, some people believe Cuban labs have biological weapons, disease germs, and toxic agents for use against the United States.

ARGUMENTS AGAINST THE EMBARGO

Nearly all of the people who argue against the embargo point out that, after 60 years, its sanctions have failed to do what it set out to do—remove Castro from power. In fact, many say the sanctions made Castro stronger and kept him in power. His constant claims the United States is an "imperialist bully" appear true.[2] Taking away the embargo removes the argument and weakens

OLD CARS

One of the most visible symbols of the US embargo can be seen on streets all over Cuba. Most Cubans cannot afford modern cars, so they are masters at patching together old American cars and inventing ways to keep them running. Most of the cars are from between the 1930s and 1950s and were in Cuba before the Castro brothers took power.

Walking through the streets of Cuba is similar to walking through an old car museum.

the Castro brothers in the eyes of the world and with their own people.

Not only does the embargo not harm the Castro brothers, critics argue, it hurts the United States. The embargo, as it is applied now, is weak. Since the United States began selling food and medicine to Cuba again in 2000, it has been one of the island's leading food suppliers. According to the New York–based US-Cuba Trade and Economic Council, US food sales to Cuba in 2014 amounted to $291 million. That number is down from $349 million in 2013 and far below the $710 million in food sold to Cuba in 2008.[3] The reason for the drop is the embargo forbids US companies to extend credit to Cuba.

As a result, Cuba buys more food from Asian, European, and Latin-American countries that will sell to Cuba on credit. In this way, the embargo has cost US businesses and farmers billions of dollars and ultimately hurt the US economy.

Perhaps the most potent argument against the embargo is that it hurts the very people it is intended to help—the Cuban people. Studies show US sanctions have significantly affected millions of Cuban citizens by adding to their poverty and sense of abandonment to their fate. Contact with Americans, not isolation from them, is exactly what Cuba needs. Some people argue a year of positive

Castro's bold stand against the United States during the embargo made him famous on the world stage.

engagement will accomplish far more than decades of embargo.

HELMS-BURTON

Complicating US policy involving Cuba is the Helms-Burton Act of 1996. At the time it was introduced, this legislation was unlike any other ever enacted pertaining to a foreign government. The act tightened the embargo in several ways. First, it said the embargo would not be lifted until Cuba paid money owed to anyone whose property was taken by the government after the revolution. It also said any individual or company who bought or built on that property in Cuba could be sued in US courts.

The most binding aspect of the law was it codified the embargo. Before 1996, the embargo was an unofficial policy. Each president renewed and followed it by choice as he saw fit. After Helms-Burton came into effect, the embargo was law. It could be stopped only by an act of

"IF YOU WANT A PEACEFUL TRANSITION TO DEMOCRACY, IS IT NOT A BETTER IDEA TO LIFT THE EMBARGO AND DROWN CASTRO'S REVOLUTION IN A FLOOD OF AMERICAN TOURISTS, AMERICAN INVESTMENTS, AMERICAN CONSUMER GOODS, AMERICAN IDEAS AND IDEALS? DOES ANYONE REALLY BELIEVE THAT CASTRO'S REVOLUTION COULD SURVIVE THE OPENING UP OF HIS COUNTRY?"[4]

—ARTHUR SCHLESINGER JR., US HISTORIAN AND SOCIAL CRITIC, 1994

Congress. The law said the embargo could end only when Cuba had a democratically elected government. With either Castro brother in power, that would never happen.

The act seemed to end any chance that discussions between Havana and Washington, DC, would ever take place. Helms-Burton required the US president to demand the United Nations approve a "mandatory international embargo."[5] That meant no one else in the world could deal with Cuba either. If any country did, they would face legal action from the United Nations. The problem was that Canada and other close allies of the United States had traded with Cuba for years. Acceptance of that clause of the act immediately caused hard feelings among the United States' closest partners.

At the time he signed the law, President Bill Clinton said he understood many of its provisions to be merely "an expression of Congress's wishes." He called some parts of the law "overly rigid" and wondered if others were even constitutional.[6] Mostly, he said, the act severely restricted the actions future presidents could take in relation to Cuba. Many critics agree and have compared the Helms-Burton Act of 1996 to the 1903 Platt Amendment.

Similar to Platt, Helms-Burton seeks to dictate to Cubans what they can and cannot do. According to authors William Ratliff and Roger Fontaine, it nurtures the "seeds of a long-smoldering resentment" in Cubans toward the United States and continues the same policies that have failed to work since the mid-1900s.[7]

"I DON'T THINK IT IS MORALLY POSSIBLE TO MAKE MATTERS WORSE IN THE HOPE SOMEHOW, SOME DAY IT WILL GET BETTER. IT'S SIMPLY NOT ACCEPTABLE TO FOLLOW A STRATEGY DESIGNED TO MAKE THE LIVES OF MOST CUBANS SO DESPERATE THAT THEY WILL RISE IN BLOODY REVOLT."[9]

—LATIN-AMERICAN ANALYST ROGER FONTAINE, 2000

In January 2015, in his State of the Union address, President Obama urged Congress to lift the trade embargo. Congress resisted the president's request, and the president himself said nothing could be done until several difficult issues were worked out. Josefina Vidal, a leading Cuban diplomat, said her nation is eager to begin the process. She said, "We know that this is the way the United States government [works], but what we believe is that we can respect each other's differences and at the same time work together on issues of common interest as neighbors."[8]

CHAPTER SIX

THE CUBAN
ECONOMY

The US embargo has been in place since 1960, but conditions in Cuba have changed dramatically over the years. Much of this change is due to the collapse of the Soviet Union in 1991. Before 1989, Cuba conducted nearly 90 percent of its trade with Soviet countries. When the Soviet Union collapsed in 1991, Castro lost more than $6 billion in annual economic assistance.[1] His dream of a shining, prosperous socialist state ended. The Soviet collapse, coupled with a tightening US embargo, forced Cuba into what Castro called "a special period in time of peace."[2] The special period was not a military conflict but an economic one.

For several years, from 1989 to the mid-1990s, Cuba experienced food and oil shortages and an intense

Before the Soviet Union fell, Castro worked closely with Soviet president Mikhail Gorbachev on economic assistance for Cuba.

economic crisis. Daily life for many Cubans became a struggle. Unemployment, poverty, and hunger increased significantly. Castro called for the Cuban people to make greater sacrifices, work harder, and complain less. The government rationed more food and clothing, many industries shut down, and people were sent to the countryside to work on civic projects or cooperative farms. Fearful these events signaled even harder times, thousands of Cubans set sail for the United States on flimsy rafts and boats.

Castro began making subtle changes in Cuba's economy. The first change was to legalize the use of the US dollar in August 1993. This allowed the economy to benefit from the money Cuban Americans sent to their relatives in Cuba. For the first time, Castro made it legal

CUBANS CARRIED AWAY ON FLYING PIGEONS

People who live in a country with a poor economy often need to find cheap and reliable ways to move around. This is why nearly everyone in Cuba rides bicycles. Many Cubans ride them to and from work, and it is not unusual for Cubans to travel more than 30 miles (50 km) on a bike in a single day. A Chinese company called Flying Pigeon makes the most common bikes in Cuba. It is estimated there are more than 800,000 Flying Pigeon bikes in Havana alone.[3] When Castro made private businesses legal in 1993, bicycle repair, spare parts, and accessories shops sprang up across the nation. Having more bikes than cars on city streets means much less air pollution from motor exhaust. But with so many bikes on busy streets, accidents are frequent.

to spend those dollars in Cuban stores. Around the same time, he established a tax system, legalized self-employment, and established farmers' markets, where growers could sell their produce to individuals or to the state and keep their own profits. In addition, Castro began converting some state-run

cooperatives to joint ventures that would be shared by the state with individual business owners. He raised prices on food, gasoline, electricity, and other goods or services that had previously been provided by the government free or at a reduced cost.

Castro did not make all of these changes happily. Many observers saw the sudden shift toward a more capitalistic approach as going against the socialist principles upon which the revolution was based. Castro said he would never do this. In 1993, he stated, "Life, reality . . . forces us to do what we would have never done otherwise . . . we must make concessions."[4] Castro later confessed in a 2005

interview that he traced many of Cuba's problems in the 2000s back to events and decisions he made during the special period.

The changes worked to some extent. By 2000, due largely to the willingness of Cubans to adapt and invent new ways to survive, Cuba's economy improved. Increased tourism and a strong trade partnership with Venezuela allowed Cuba to more than double its imports and carry out multibillion-dollar improvements across the island. Since 2008, these improvements, as well as the high price of nickel—one of Cuba's more valuable natural resources—have helped Cubans recover some of the standards of living they had in place before the fall of the Soviet Union.

In speeches and actions since 2008, Raúl has shown he wants to shift away from the old, rigid socialist system his brother imposed. Raúl approved programs allowing private farmers to work plots of public land. He also allowed people to sell used cars and opened access to some types of previously prohibited consumer goods, such as cell phones, computers, and home appliances. While these actions are symbolically important, they

Cubans were given one month's share of food by the government during the economic crisis.

have, so far, had little effect on overall economic growth. A government restriction on who can have access to supplies of goods and labor discourages hiring and reduces the profits businesses can earn. Free enterprise in Cuba is still hampered by high taxes, limited access to transportation and credit, and a number of government regulations and restrictions.

The current Cuban economy is a mixture of socialism and capitalism. Raúl has long been an admirer of China and Vietnam, two socialist nations that have thrived under a one-party system of government. As Fidel's influence fades and Raúl's continues to grow, a less rigid attachment to ideas of the past is becoming the norm rather than the exception.

Raúl wants to move toward a more open and free economy, one that is a partially state-run, mixed-market, and socialist economy.

CHAPTER SEVEN

THE HUMAN
RIGHTS
QUESTION

O ne of the remaining issues standing in the way of ending the US trade embargo and opening the door to a healthy relationship with Cuba is human rights. Almost no one denies Cuba's citizens lack many basic political and economic freedoms. The list of offenses is long and dates back many years.

The United States has diplomatic ties with nations that have worse human rights records than Cuba. These nations include China and Vietnam. Freedom House, an independent group that monitors human rights in countries around the world, rates Saudi Arabia, Bahrain,

A group of Cuban dissidents celebrate in the streets after a well-known member of their group is released from jail.

and Jordan as not free nations. Yet the US government considers these countries friends and allies.

In 1975, the United States supported Joseph Mobutu, president of the Democratic Republic of the Congo—now Zaire. Despite Mobutu's dictatorship, the US government gave him millions of dollars during Zaire's civil war. President Carter stated the United States knew of Mobutu's brutality. He said, "But our friendship and aid historically for Zaire has not been predicated on their perfection in dealing with human rights."[1] The statement made many human rights activists wonder why the United States overlooked crimes against humanity in Africa, yet condemned far lesser violations in Cuba. Similar questions arose in the 1980s when the US government maintained relations with violent, oppressive leaders in Argentina

RADIO MARTÍ

Named for Cuba's most beloved founding father, Jose Martí, Radio Martí began radio broadcasting on May 20, 1985, Cuba's Independence Day. The station, headquartered in Miami, is operated with US government funds and broadcasts news and information Cubans cannot get any other way. The Cuban government strongly objects to Radio Martí, while the Cuban-American community strongly supports it. The station now broadcasts both radio and television programs, and much of the programming is available online. Since Internet access is severely limited in Cuba, Radio Martí also puts its programs on flash drives and distributes them on the island.

and Chile but continued to condemn Cuba for holding
political prisoners.

Cuba's treatment of protesters and rebels became
a major issue in 2003. That year, School of the Americas
Watch, a group that monitors human rights throughout
Latin American and the Caribbean, reported Castro
had arrested dozens of rebels protesting against the
government in Cuba. The group called the crackdown "the
worst we've seen in a decade or more."

Cuban laws allow the government to arrest anyone
who distributes "subversive materials" or "who put
themselves at the service of the power that is attacking
our people."[2] Defenders of Cuba's restrictive laws admit
that by democratic standards, the laws may violate
some freedoms of association and expression. But these
defenders are quick to point out the United States has
similar laws making it illegal for anyone to accept money
from or provide aid to terrorists or enemies. Cuba, they say,
is only taking the same actions.

Castro's government has long asserted he arrested
only terrorists and those people who sought to disturb
the peace and stability in Cuba. Castro blamed "the

Cuban American terrorist mafia" in Florida and Cuban Americans who visited relatives in Cuba for encouraging civil disobedience and spreading discontent among the population.[3]

Castro cited the United States Interests Section in Havana as another source of concern. This office opened in Cuba in 1977 after President Carter expressed an interest in normalizing relations with Cuba. It was not an embassy but simply a place where US representatives could meet with Cubans to discuss issues and concerns. Castro objected to activities by staff members, believing they spread antigovernment materials and organized rebels to stage illegal demonstrations. In 2003, Castro clamped down on protesters and restricted travel by diplomats on the island.

OPENING DOORS

The number of political prisoners in Cuba was reduced from 283 at the end of 2006 to 230 in February 2008. Some people believe this is evidence of Cuba's declining repression. But other political activists insist the overall situation has not improved. The Cuban government detained more than 300 people for short periods in 2007.[4]

According to a 2014 Human Rights Watch report, Cuba has eased some of its former policies in recent years. Between 2010 and 2011, Cuban authorities released more political prisoners and relied less on long-term prison sentences to control rebels. The same report, however, noted Cuba still uses other methods to control its citizens. Random arrests and short-term lockups have increased significantly in recent years. Fear of arrest and intimidation prevents human rights leaders, independent journalists, and others in Cuba from gathering or moving about freely. Arrests often happen before marches or meetings where people plan to gather to discuss politics. Rebels are often beaten, threatened, or held in solitary confinement for hours or days.

Perhaps nothing else in the modern world represents freedom more than the Internet, where free speech and creative expression flourish.

"THE GOOD WILL EXPRESSED BY THE CUBAN AUTHORITIES WITH THIS SERIES OF RELEASES MUST ABSOLUTELY TRANSLATE INTO THE IMPLEMENTATION OF A NEW HUMAN RIGHTS AGENDA. RESPECT FOR FREEDOM OF EXPRESSION, ASSEMBLY AND ASSOCIATION MUST BE THE NEXT STEP IF THE CUBAN AUTHORITIES WANT TO KEEP THEIR CREDIBILITY IN THE FACE OF A WORLD WHICH IS WATCHING THEM."[5]

—ERIKA GUEVARA ROSAS, AMERICAS DIRECTOR AT AMNESTY INTERNATIONAL, 2015

In Cuba, however, the government tightly controls all standard media outlets—radio, television, newspapers, and the Internet—and therefore limits access to outside information. Since only approximately 4 percent of Cuban homes have Internet access of any kind, the government has not had to control much digital information.[6] Still, when a group of Cuban journalists started a digital news site in 2014, the government immediately blocked it. The government has taken similar steps to restrict other digital freedom of speech activities, such as blogging, e-mail, and messaging. Cuba's state-run newspaper has blamed the government's slow progress toward cyber equality on what it calls "Washington's punitive policy toward Havana," also known as the embargo.[7]

By the time President Obama stated in 2014 that he intended to reconnect with Cuba and called on Congress to end the embargo, negative attitudes in Cuba had already begun changing. When the Cuban government announced it was willing to take steps to make the Internet more readily available, President Obama responded that the United States would make it easier for US technology companies to do business in Cuba in the near future. How much control the government will give up is unknown. Bloggers in Cuba, for example, are still censored and subject to arrest if they criticize the government.

Representatives for the United States and Cuba agreed in March 2015 to meet at a future date to discuss human rights questions. Most political scientists agree such a meeting would never have happened a few years earlier and signal a desire by Cuba to improve its human rights record. As US diplomat John Caulfield said, "The very fact, I think, that Cuba is in a formal process where they agreed to talk about human rights . . . makes it more difficult for them to do the heavy-handed stuff they've done in the past."[8]

Students gather around a free Internet portal outside a business center in Havana.

CHAPTER EIGHT

PAY IT BACK,
GIVE IT BACK

Two major issues must be resolved before the United States will lift its trade embargo against Cuba. Americans want reparations in the form of the millions of dollars of US property that was seized in Cuba and nationalized by Castro's government beginning in the 1960s. The Cuban government wants the United States to give back the land at Guantánamo Bay Naval Base. Each of these issues is an economically, emotionally, and politically complicated knot. Unraveling them will require firm diplomatic skills and willingness to compromise from both sides.

The US Congress established a Cuban Claims Program in October 1964. This program set up a

The United States and Cuba both want resolutions before the embargo is lifted, including a decision about the land housing Guantánamo Bay Naval Base.

GUANTÁNAMO BAY NAVAL BASE

Guantánamo Bay Naval Base is a 45-square-mile (120 sq km) military base located in southeastern Cuba. As part of the Platt Amendment in 1903, the United States agreed to lease the land for approximately $4,085 per year.[2] Since the Castros' government takeover in 1959, Cuba has refused to accept the payment. They claim the US presence at the base is "illegal and on land occupied against the will of the Cuban people."[3] After the September 11 terrorist attacks in 2001, part of the base was set aside as a place to hold prisoners captured in the United States' war on terrorism, sparking even more controversy in Cuba and around the world. Both nations guard the base's 17-mile (30 km) border.

commission to figure out who had unpaid claims and how much Cuba owed them. Between 1966 and 1972, the Foreign Claims Settlement Commission reviewed claims from US citizens and companies. It determined the total amount of money owed for those claims was $1.8 billion.[1] Various attempts by individuals and companies to get Cuba to pay back the money have failed.

Over the years, the Castros tried to convince Cubans reengagement with the United States would require them to give up property that was abandoned by fleeing exiles or confiscated after the revolution. Cubans were told any agreement with the United States would likely mean they would have to give up money, homes, businesses, jobs, and security. Many Cubans who achieved lower middle class status and housing during and after the revolution fear they will lose all of their belongings if an agreement is reached. They believe they will return to lives of poverty.

Cuban Americans frequently describe the pain and suffering they have endured by being forced from their native country. Much of this pain is caused by the realization the Castros took over the property and possessions they left behind. The Helms-Burton Act of 1996 more tightly connected these specific claims to the trade embargo by making repayment a requirement for the sanctions to be lifted.

The Helms-Burton Act threatened to punish any foreign-based companies that bought or leased confiscated property. Legal experts have pointed out the difficulty US courts would have trying to take action against non-Americans. Also, in some cases, those businesses might be owned by some of the United States' closest allies, such as Canada and the European Union.

With the nation's economic woes, Cuba will have a hard time finding the billions of dollars needed to pay people back. As one Cuban-American writer asked, "What good would monetary compensation be when our family, friends, and compatriots continue to suffer?"[4] Perhaps, many say, it would be best to halt the constant demands for financial compensation and instead work for the return of democracy to Cuba. Maybe once Cuba is free and back on its feet financially, it may be possible to seek repayment through legal channels.

For their part, the Castros claim Cuba is owed more than $100 billion in damages caused by the US embargo.[5] In a January 2015 speech, Raúl repeated that claim, saying the United States must agree to a "just compensation to our people for the human and economic damage that they've suffered."[6] It is likely, according to some observers, such statements are diplomatic maneuvering in preparation for the negotiations Cuba knows are coming soon.

GUANTÁNAMO BAY NAVAL BASE

Perhaps there is no better symbol of the tense relationship between the United States and Cuba than Guantánamo Bay Naval Base. The base forms a 17-mile (30 km) border between Cuban land and US land and is lined with razor wire and land mines.

Guantánamo Bay is heavily guarded around its perimeter.

Cuba was forced to lease the land housing the base
to the United States in 1903, and it has been a point
of controversy and division ever since. The base was
established originally as a place where US ships could
refuel while watching the Caribbean Sea. After the Castros
took control of the government and Cuba joined with the
Soviet Union, the base became a way for the United States

to show Cuba and the Soviet Union it had no intention of backing down.

Cuba no longer poses a direct threat to the United States. As one high-ranking officer said, "Guantánamo serves no military purpose, affords no strategic advantage. . . . The place exists solely as a product of a bureaucratic inertia."[7] In other words, removing it requires far more effort than simply leaving it as it is.

Guantánamo Bay detention camp's main purpose today is as a place for the US government to house its most dangerous political prisoners. In that respect, Guantánamo's greatest value is that US laws and moral codes are not in effect there. According to author Jonathan Hansen, the base has caused damage to US military operations and its international reputation. As Castro once said, "The base is needed to humiliate and to do the dirty work that occurs there."

Raúl said in January 2015 that normalizing relations between Cuba and the United States "will not be possible while the blockade still exists, while they don't give back the territory illegally occupied by the Guantánamo naval base." And most Cubans feel the same way. As one Cuban citizen said, "How can we be friends with a country that still squats on our land?"[9]

Yet giving Guantánamo back to Cuba may be harder than it appears. The legal and political snarl surrounding the base in its current state as a detention camp will be extremely difficult to unravel. And, according to White House sources, even if the detention camp is closed, the base will remain a US possession. Many agree Guantánamo Bay Naval Base will never close no matter how many demands the Cubans make. They point out the base's use and purpose has changed many times over the years. Even if the base stays a US possession, it is likely a change will happen again.

FROM THE
HEADLINES

DETENTION CAMP

Since it opened in 2002, the detention camp at Guantánamo Bay Naval Base in Cuba has continued to make headlines. Despite protests and objections from the United Nations and many human rights groups, the detention camp still holds approximately 122 detainees.[10] Most of them were captured during the United States' war on terrorism, which started after the September 11, 2001, attacks on the World Trade Center and other targets.

During his 2008 campaign, President Obama promised to close the detention camp within one year of his election. Yet, many years later, the detention camp and the prisoners are still there. "It is a hard problem," the president has admitted. "It's a tough legal problem. It's a tough security problem."[11]

Castro and others have pointed out the United States has long accused him of human rights violations, yet they impart similar violations at the detention camp on Cuban soil. One major issue is many of the prisoners are held without having been formally charged with any crime, other than the fact they are enemies of the United States. International law says these prisoners have a right to some sort of trial or legal process, but no one can agree on what that process might be. Another problem is many of the prisoners have been cleared for release. Yet their home countries,

Reports of routine mistreatment of prisoners, particularly the use of torture, have increased pressure on the United States to close the facility.

for one reason or another, refuse to accept them. Making a hard problem even harder is the fact US Congress passed measures forbidding prisoners from being moved to US soil.

CHAPTER NINE

A BRIGHTER
FUTURE

O ver the years, many people have speculated about the future of US-Cuba relations. Latin American scholar Jamie Suchlicki took a dark view of the future in his 2002 book, *Cuba: From Columbus to Castro and Beyond*. In the book, Castro, who is old, sick, and bitter after years of struggling against the United States, makes a momentous decision. He decides to make a grand exit from politics by luring the United States into a catastrophic battle. Castro orders his military to simultaneously attack Guantánamo Bay Naval Base and Miami. As Castro expects, the massive counterattack by the United States invades Cuba. He, Raúl, and the thousands of Cubans who rally to Castro's call to arms are killed making a last stand against the

No one is sure how a future Cuba without the Castro brothers will look.

US armies. The United States is left to clean up, rebuild, and occupy a devastated, empty island.

Of his book, Suchlicki has said, "This unlikely, and for many people unthinkable . . . scenario should be considered, given Castro's anti-Americanism, failing revolution, and historical mind-set." After all, Suchlicki points out, Castro once expressed a wish for "the Cuban island to sink into the ocean before surrendering to US imperialism."[1]

Many people have imagined what Cuba's future would be like without the Castros. As early as 2007, as a presidential candidate, Barack Obama promised if he were elected, his administration would engage Cuba more openly. In fact, he said it would be "the foremost

ZUNZUNEO—CUBAN TWITTER

US agents working for the United States Agency for International Development (USAID), an agency that seeks to promote democracy in Cuba developed a secret program in 2009. They hired private companies to develop a basic Twitter-style program that allowed Cubans to send free text messages to each other. The messages could not be controlled or traced by Cuban authorities. ZunZuneo, which is Cuban slang for the sound a hummingbird makes, began operation in September 2010. At its peak, the program had 40,000 subscribers.[2] That is when the US government decided to stop funding the program. ZunZuneo vanished suddenly in mid-2011, leaving thousands of its mostly young users wondering where it had gone. Few of them realized they had been part of a US program to provide them with more freedom of expression than they had ever known.

objective of our policy."[3] Since then, events have occurred that few people could have imagined a decade ago.

To begin, Raúl took control of the Cuban government in 2008. One of his first moves was to name José Ramón Machado Ventura as the first vice president of the Council of State. Prior to Ventura, Raúl had held the position since 1976. Ventura is a close friend and confident of Raúl, and the position makes him the official successor to Raúl, according to the Cuban constitution. Many people read this move as a sign the brothers hope the government will not change after they are gone. However, since taking control in 2008, Raúl has made a number of changes. Like President Obama, Raúl has made statements revealing his desire to depart from the past. In December 2010, he admitted the Communist Party had failed in a number of ways. He then asked citizens to be more openly critical of Cuba's government than they had in the past. Such a request opposes the iron grip he and Fidel have always kept on freedom of speech and on critics who dared to challenge them.

No one knows what the transition period from the Castros to the next phase of Cuban history will be like.

ALAN GROSS AND THE CUBAN FIVE

American Alan Gross was arrested in 2009 for delivering cell phones and other communications equipment to residents of a small Jewish community in Cuba. Gross spent nearly five years in a Cuban prison before he was released in December 2014. At about the same time, the United States released three Cubans convicted for spying in 2001. They were part of a group known as the "Cuban Five," two of whom were released earlier. The group was arrested for collecting information about Cuban-American exile leaders and US military bases. The exchange of the three spies for Gross took place as a goodwill gesture, part of a larger effort that began when President Obama and Raúl announced their agreement to reestablish diplomatic relations.

One factor that must inevitably change in US-Cuba relations has to do with Cuban Americans. To Latin-American scholar and writer Lars Schoultz, Cuban Americans' ability to influence US politics makes them a potent power for change. Until now, they have continued to demand that the United States react with unrelenting hostility to every action Cuba's government takes. Until recently, Cuba's leaders have responded in exactly the same spirit. For the situation to shift, Schoultz has said Cuban Americans need to cast their ballots for candidates who do not "promise to be more vigorous in their hostility toward Cuba's revolutionary government."[4]

Youth, according to historian Richard Gott, may be Cuba's real salvation. Over the past several decades, Fidel surrounded himself with young people and promoted them to positions in the government. Although the current leadership is still made up of "white-bearded guerrilla fighters from the 1950's . . . young graduates from the island's universities and technical schools" are replacing them. These young leaders are not "controlled by veterans from the revolutionary war" but are forward thinking and creative. Gott says "Castro's Revolution put Cuba on the map," and he inspired in the Cuban people "a real sense of pride in their nation."[5]

This pride, according to many historians and observers, is what generations of Americans have failed to understand about Cuba. Cuba does not want another nation telling them how they must act. Cubans want to make their own decisions, choose their own leaders, and create their own future. The challenge for US policymakers is to accept any government or leader Cubans decide they want—even if it is not a US-style democracy.

In the end, Cubans simply want respect. Fidel made this clear in 1959. He said, "The Cuban government and the Cuban people are anxious to live in peace and harmony with the government and the people of the United States; and they are also desirous of intensifying their diplomatic and economic relations, but on a basis of mutual respect."[6] Later, Castro sent a private message to President Kennedy. It said, "I seriously hope . . . that Cuba and the United States can eventually sit down in an atmosphere of good will and mutual respect and negotiate our differences."[7] But as history shows, speaking and acting respectfully have not often been a part of the United States' policy toward Cuba. As Raúl said in December 2013, "If we really want to make progress in bilateral relations, we have to learn to respect each other's differences and get used to living peacefully with them. Otherwise, no. We are ready for another 55 years like the last."[8]

President Obama has already started taking steps toward ending the trade embargo. One of the hurdles he has been working to remove includes making travel to and from Cuba easier. In May 2015, for instance, the US Department of the Treasury issued licenses to at least two

US companies to begin regular ferryboat service to and from Cuba. The president also has executive foreign policy powers at his disposal. Under these constitutional powers he can send and receive ambassadors. In his final months in office, President Obama appeared willing to establish better relations with Cuba.

In the end, several different federal laws, including the Helms-Burton Act and the Trading with the Enemy Act, still support the embargo. Only Congress can change those laws. It is unlikely Congress will approve lifting the embargo without a fight. Members of Congress vowed they would block any attempts by the president to change the law.

Presidential candidates had to carefully consider their stand on the situation in Cuba as they campaigned for election in 2016. Cuban Americans traditionally have not supported candidates who want to end the embargo or become friendly with the Castros. But recent polls show these old attitudes are changing. In 1991, a poll showed 87 percent of Cuban Americans were in favor of continuing the embargo.[10] In 2014, the same poll revealed only 48 percent still supported the embargo.[11]

FROM THE
HEADLINES

LET'S GET TOGETHER

On December 17, 2014, President Obama and Raúl Castro surprised the world with their historic announcement that Cuba and the United States were restoring diplomatic relations. Although the announcement seemed to come out of nowhere, it did not just happen. It was the result of 18 months of secret discussions in Canada and in Vatican City, Italy.

US-Cuba relations began to thaw in 2009, when both US and Cuban leaders made statements that they wished for a better situation between the two nations. In 2013, at memorial ceremonies in South Africa for Nelson Mandela, Raúl and President Obama shook hands, smiled, and spoke briefly. Many saw this momentary meeting as a sign the two nations were moving closer together.

In March 2014, when President Obama visited Vatican City, he and Pope Francis discussed the possibility of ending the division between Cuba and the United States. Several months later, Pope Francis sent letters to Raúl and Obama urging them to send representatives to Vatican City to engage in talks. A series of nine secret meetings followed in Vatican City, and Canada, where US and Cuban leaders discussed issues and made plans for future connections.

The two leaders met and had an hour-long discussion, the first such meeting since 1959.

A historic series of steps began at noon on December 17, 2014, when Obama and Raúl appeared before their respective nations to simultaneously announce an agreement to restore diplomatic relations. Delegations from both nations met in Havana in January 2015 and again in April at the Summit of the Americas in Panama. President Obama announced later the removal of Cuba from the United States' list of nations that support terrorism. That important step cleared the way for even more actions, such as opening embassies in each other's capitols.

Overall, national popular opinion in 2015 has shifted in favor of ending the embargo. At least one leading Republican, Kentucky Senator Rand Paul, supports better relations with Cuba. Others appear ready to shift their attitude toward Cuba, too. Yet Senator Marco Rubio, of Florida, promises to oppose any government moves to establish diplomatic ties with Cuba.

Perhaps in the future, the United States and Cuba may finally become friendlier neighbors. Clearly, a great deal of work remains to repair decades of hard feelings, but both sides appear eager to continue the journey that has already begun.

The key to finally opening the door to neighborly relations may not be as complicated as it sometimes appears. The door is not fully open yet, but people are meeting and talking. The decades–long embargo and travel ban are still in place, but both sides have agreed to allow educational and people-to-people visits. The tide appears to be turning. In the end, the real reconciliation will not be about the differences between Cubans and Americans but the similarities they share.

A Cuban citizen hangs an American flag and a Cuban flag from his balcony after the announcement of Castro and Obama's meeting in 2014.

ESSENTIAL
FACTS

MAJOR EVENTS

- In 1898, the United States defeats Spain in the Spanish-American War, leaving the United States in control of Cuba and several other territories.

- In 1959, Fidel Castro's revolution defeats Fulgencio Batista and Castro takes control of Cuba.

- In 1962, Soviet missiles in Cuba nearly bring the world to war.

- In 2015, the United States and Cuba announce resumption of diplomatic relations.

KEY PLAYERS

- Fidel Castro serves as prime minister of Cuba from 1959 to 1976 and president from 1976 to 2008. He is a ruthless dictator.

- Raúl Castro serves as minister of the armed forces from 1959 to 2008. He holds several other positions in the Cuban government but is always considered second in power behind Fidel. Raúl assumes the role of president after Fidel resigns due to ill health in 2008.

- The Cuban-American community is composed of approximately 2.1 million Cubans in the United States, mostly living in Miami, Florida. They are traditionally opposed to the Castros and have influenced US politics for many years.

IMPACT ON SOCIETY

The long and troubled relationship between the United States and Cuba has affected the lives of millions in both nations and around the world. The US trade embargo has imposed untold suffering on the Cuban people and driven many people to attempt crossing the dangerous Florida Straits to find better lives in the United States. This mass migration of people has created the large Cuban community in exile that both divides and unites the United States and Cuba.

QUOTE

"The problem is, of course, that most people do not want a neighboring power to lift them up, regardless of how well intentioned the effort might be, and Cuba's revolutionary generation grew up in a society that left it particularly opposed to uplifting by the United States."

—Lars Schoultz, author, historian, and past president of the Latin American Studies Association

GLOSSARY

ANNEXATION
To take as one's own, as in one country taking another as a colony or territory.

COOPERATIVE FARM
A farm run by a group of people who share machinery, labor, and produce.

DICTATOR
One who takes power by force and holds power by imposing his or her will upon others.

DUE PROCESS
The official and proper way of doing things in a legal case.

EMBARGO
A form of sanction in which one nation refuses to trade or deal with another nation and encourages other nations to do the same.

EMBASSY
The building where an ambassador lives and works.

GUERRILLA

A soldier who is often a rebel who seeks to disrupt or destroy an established government or large military force.

PAROLE

Permission given to a prisoner to leave prison early as a reward for behavior.

PROPAGANDA

Information that persuades or pressures others.

REGIME

A government in power.

SANCTION

An order given to force a country to obey international laws.

SOCIALISM

An economic theory or system in which the community owns the means of production, distribution, and exchange collectively, usually through the state.

SOVEREIGNTY

Freedom from control by another nation.

ADDITIONAL
RESOURCES

SELECTED BIBLIOGRAPHY

Castro, Fidel. *My Life: Fidel Castro*. London: Allen Lane, 2007. Print.

Gott, Richard. *Cuba: A New History*. New Haven, CT: Yale UP, 2004. Print.

Ratliff, William, and Roger Fontaine. *A Strategic Flip-Flop in the Caribbean: Lift the Embargo on Cuba*. Stanford, CA: Stanford, 2000. Print.

Schoultz, Lars. *That Infernal Little Cuban Republic: The United States and the Cuban Revolution*. Chapel Hill, NC: U of North Carolina P, 2009. Print.

FURTHER READINGS

Gitlin, Martin. *US Sanctions on Cuba*. Minneapolis: Abdo, 2011. Print.

Sweig, Julia E. *Cuba: What Everyone Needs to Know*. New York: Oxford UP, 2012. Print.

WEBSITES

To learn more about Special Reports, visit **booklinks.abdopublishing.com**. These links are routinely monitored and updated to provide the most current information available.

FOR MORE INFORMATION

For more information on this subject, contact or visit the following organizations:

Cuban American National Foundation (CANF)
2147 SW Eighth Street
Miami, FL 33135
305-592-7768
http://canf.org/contact
The Cuban American National Foundation (CANF) is a nonprofit organization dedicated to advancing freedom and democracy in Cuba. CANF is the largest Cuban organization to represent part of the Cuban exile community.

USAID Cuba
Information Center, US Agency for International Development
Ronald Reagan Building
Washington, DC 20523
202-712-4810 or 202-712-0000
http://www.usaid.gov/where-we-work/latin-american-and-caribbean/cuba
The United States Agency for International Development (USAID) provides funds to various organizations in an effort to bring about change to the Cuban government. USAID supports the peaceful transition to democracy in Cuba.

SOURCE
NOTES

CHAPTER 1. A COLD WAR SHOWDOWN

1. Leon Neyfakh. "Cuba, You Owe Us $7 Billion." *Boston Globe*. Boston Globe Media Partners, 18 Apr. 2014. Web. 10 June 2015.

2. Richard Gott. *Cuba: A New History*. New Haven, CT: Yale UP, 2004. Print. 194.

3. Jim Rasenberger. *The Brilliant Disaster: JFK, Castro, and America's Doomed Invasion of Cuba's Bay of Pigs*. New York: Scribner, 2011. Print. 379–380.

4. "Cuban Missile Crisis." *History*. A&E Television Networks, 2015. Web. 10 June 2015.

5. James G. Blight and Philip Brenner. *Sad and Luminous Days: Cuba's Struggle With the Superpowers after the Missile Crisis*. Lanham, MD: Rowman & Littlefield, 2002. Print. 189.

6. Sebastian Balfour. *Castro*. Harlow, England: Pearson Longman, 2009. Print. 64.

CHAPTER 2. UNEASY NEIGHBORS

1. Thomas Jefferson. "Letter to James Monroe, October 24, 1823." *Mount Holyoke College*. Mount Holyoke College, 2008. Web. 10 June 2015.

2. "Cuban Liberty, American License." *New York Times*. New York Times Company, 27 Sept. 1981. Web. 10 June 2015.

3. Lars Schoultz. *That Infernal Little Cuban Republic: The United States and the Cuban Revolution*. Chapel Hill, NC: U of North Carolina P, 2009. Print. 26.

4. Richard Gott. *Cuba: A New History*. New Haven, CT: Yale UP, 2004. Print. 147–150.

5. Lars Schoultz. *That Infernal Little Cuban Republic: The United States and the Cuban Revolution*. Chapel Hill, NC: U of North Carolina P, 2009. Print. 553.

CHAPTER 3. FIDEL CASTRO'S SUPPORTERS

1. William Ratliff and Roger Fontaine. *A Strategic Flip-Flop in the Caribbean: Lift the Embargo on Cuba*. Stanford, CA: Stanford, 2000. Print. 27.

2. Steven Nelson. "Joanne Chesimard, Fugitive Living in Cuba, Named to FBI 'Most Wanted Terrorists' List." *US News*. US News and World Report, 2 May 2013. Web. 10 June 2015.

3. Richard Gott. *Cuba: A New History*. New Haven, CT: Yale UP, 2004. Print. 188–189.

4. William Ratliff and Roger Fontaine. *A Strategic Flip-Flop in the Caribbean: Lift the Embargo on Cuba*. Stanford, CA: Stanford, 2000. Print. 7.

5. Ibid. 46–47.

6. Richard Gott. *Cuba: A New History.* New Haven, CT: Yale UP, 2004. Print. 324–325.

7. Carlos Franqui. *Diary of the Cuban Revolution.* New York: Viking, 1980. Print. 278.

CHAPTER 4. TRAVELING TO AND FROM CUBA

1. "Hispanic or Latino By Type: 2010." *United States Census Bureau.* US Census Bureau, 2010. Web. 10 June 2015.

2. Ann Louise Bardach. "Why Are Cubans So Special?" *New York Times.* New York Times Company, 29 Jan. 2015. Web. 10 June 2015.

3. Richard Gott. *Cuba: A New History.* New Haven, CT: Yale UP, 2004. Print. 212.

4. "The Cuban Children's Exodus." *PedroPan.org.* Operation Pedro Pan Group, 2009. Web. 10 June 2015.

5. Monte Reel. "Florida Is the New Front Line in the Battle for Venezuela." *Bloomberg Business.* Bloomberg, 31 Mar. 2015. Web. 10 June 2015.

6. "Timeline." *Frontline.* WGBH Educational Foundation, 2014. Web. 10 June 2015.

7. Yvonne M. Conde. *Operation Pedro Pan: The Untold Exodus of 14,048 Cuban Children.* New York: Routledge, 1999. Print. 180.

8. Robert B. Kent. *Latin America: Regions and People.* New York: Guilford, 2006. Print. 380.

9. "The Cuban Refugee Problem in Perspective, 1959–1980." *Heritage Foundation.* Heritage Foundation, 18 July 1980. Web. 10 June 2015.

10. Samuel Solivan. *Spirit, Pathos and Liberation: Toward an Hispanic Pentecostal Theology.* Sheffield, England: Sheffield Academic, 1998. Print. 18.

11. Richard Gott. *Cuba: A New History.* New Haven, CT: Yale UP, 2004. Print. 214.

12. Ann Louise Bardach. "Why Are Cubans So Special?" *New York Times.* New York Times Company, 29 Jan. 2015. Web. 10 June 2015.

13. Lars Schoultz. *That Infernal Little Cuban Republic: The United States and the Cuban Revolution.* Chapel Hill, NC: U of North Carolina P, 2009. Print. 543–545.

14. Ibid.

15. Amy Francis, ed. *The US Policy on Cuba.* Detroit: Greenhaven, 2009. Print. 76, 78.

16. Jaime Suchlicki, "Getting Ready for Life after Castro." *Democracy Lab.* Foreign Policy, 11 May 2012. Web. 10 June 2015.

CHAPTER 5. THE EMBARGO DEBATE

1. "Cuban Democracy Act 'CDA'." *US Department of the Treasury.* US Department of the Treasury, n.d. Web. 10 June 2015.

2. William Ratliff and Roger Fontaine. *A Strategic Flip-Flop in the Caribbean: Lift the Embargo on Cuba.* Stanford, CA: Stanford, 2000. Print. 5–7.

3. "As US Food Sales to Cuba Slow, Farmers Seek End to Embargo." *Voice of America.* VOANews.com, 6 Feb. 2015. Web. 10 June 2015.

4. Arthur Schlesinger, Jr. "US Should Lift Its Embargo on Cuba, Too." *Deseret News.* DeseretNews.com, 14 Apr. 1994. Web. 10 June 2015.

5. "Title 22—Foreign Relations and Intercourse." *Legal Information Institute.* Cornell University Law School, 4 Jan. 2012. Web. 10 June 2015.

6. Lars Schoultz. *That Infernal Little Cuban Republic: The United States and the Cuban Revolution.* Chapel Hill, NC: U of North Carolina P, 2009. Print. 485.

SOURCE NOTES
CONTINUED

7. William Ratliff and Roger Fontaine. *A Strategic Flip-Flop in the Caribbean: Lift the Embargo on Cuba*. Stanford, CA: Stanford, 2000. Print. 36–38.

8. Jim Avila and Jordyn Phelps. "US-Cuba Relations: Stage Set for Historic Meeting Between Obama and Castro." *ABC News*. ABC News, 31 Mar. 2015. Web. 10 June 2015.

9. Lars Schoultz. *That Infernal Little Cuban Republic: The United States and the Cuban Revolution*. Chapel Hill, NC: U of North Carolina P, 2009. Print. 499.

CHAPTER 6. THE CUBAN ECONOMY

1. Lars Schoultz. *That Infernal Little Cuban Republic: The United States and the Cuban Revolution*. Chapel Hill, NC: U of North Carolina P, 2009. Print. 428.

2. Richard Gott. *Cuba: A New History*. New Haven, CT: Yale UP, 2004. Print. 289.

3. Martha Hostetter, ed. *Cuba*. Bronx, NY: H.W. Wilson, 2001. Print. 87.

4. Ibid. 57.

5. Ibid. 59.

6. Ibid. 94.

CHAPTER 7. THE HUMAN RIGHTS QUESTION

1. Lars Schoultz. *That Infernal Little Cuban Republic: The United States and the Cuban Revolution*. Chapel Hill, NC: U of North Carolina P, 2009. Print. 308.

2. Ibid. 536–538.

3. Ibid. 515.

4. Mark P. Sullivan. "Cuba's Political Succession: From Fidel to Raúl Castro." *CRS Report for Congress*. Federation of American Scientists, 29 Feb. 2008. Web. 10 June 2015.

5. "Cuba: Prisoner Releases Must Lead to New Environment for Freedoms." *Amnesty International*. Amnesty International, 8 Jan. 2015. Web. 10 June 2015.

6. Brad Stone. "Airbnb Is Now Available in Cuba." *BloombergBusiness*. Bloomberg, 2 Apr. 2015. Web. 10 June 2015.

7. "Cuba's Promising New Online Voices." *New York Times*. New York Times Company, 23 Dec. 2014. Web. 10 June 2015.

8. Michael Weissenstein and Andrea Rodriquez. "Cuba, US to Launch Human Rights Dialogue Tuesday." *Yahoo! News*. Associated Press, 26 Mar. 2015. Web. 10 June 2015.

CHAPTER 8. PAY IT BACK, GIVE IT BACK

1. "Key Events—US Property Claims." *Certified Cuban Claims*. Certified Cuban Claims, n.d. Web. 10 June 2015.

2. "Guantanamo Bay Naval Station Fast Facts." *CNN*. Cable News Network, 20 Feb. 2015. Web. 10 June 2015.

3. Fidel Castro. *My Life: Fidel Castro*. London: Allen Lane, 2007. Print. 286.

4. Amy Francis, ed. *The US Policy on Cuba*. Detroit: Greenhaven, 2009. Print. 59.

5. "Legal Claims Over Assets Taken by Cuban Government." *The Law Offices of Michael D. Stewart*. Law Offices of Michael Stewart, 23 Dec. 2014. Web. 10 June 2015.

6. Javier Cordoba and Michael Weissenstein. "Raúl Castro: US Must Return Guantánamo for Normal Relations." *Miami Herald*. Miami Herald, 28 Jan. 2015. Web. 10 June 2015.

7. Jonathan M. Hansen. *Guantánamo: An American History*. New York: Hill and Wang, 2011. Print. 356.

8. Ibid. 347.

9. Georgia Birch. "Guantánamo Residents: 'How Can Cuba Talk to the US While They Occupy Our Land?'" *Telegraph*. Telegraph Media Group, 3 Apr. 2015. Web. 10 June 2015.

10. David Welna. "Senate Republicans Move to Block Further Transfers from Gitmo." *NPR*. NPR, 15 Jan. 2015. Web. 10 June 2015.

11. David Jackson. "Obama Calls Gitmo 'A Hard Problem.'" *USA Today*. USAToday.com, 29 May 2014. Web. 10 June 2015.

CHAPTER 9. A BRIGHTER FUTURE

1. Jaime Suchlicki. *Cuba: From Columbus to Castro and Beyond*. Washington, DC: Brassey's, 2002. Print. 218–219.

2. Desmond Butler, Jack Gillum, and Alberto Arce. "US Secretly Created 'Cuban Twitter' to Stir Unrest." *The Big Story*. Associated Press, 4 Apr. 2014. Web. 10 June 2015.

3. William M. LeoGrande and Peter Kornbluh. *Back Channel to Cuba: The Hidden History of Negotiations Between Washington and Havana*. Chapel Hill, NC: U of North Carolina P, 2014. Print. 368.

4. Lars Schoultz. *That Infernal Little Cuban Republic: The United States and the Cuban Revolution*. Chapel Hill, NC: U of North Carolina P, 2009. Print. 564.

5. Richard Gott. *Cuba: A New History*. New Haven, CT: Yale UP, 2004. Print. 318.

6. Lars Schoultz. *That Infernal Little Cuban Republic: The United States and the Cuban Revolution*. Chapel Hill, NC: U of North Carolina P, 2009. Print. 554.

7. "Message from Fidel Castro to Lyndon Johnson." *National Security Archive*. National Security Archive, 12 Feb. 1964. Web. 10 June 2015.

8. "Cuba's Raúl Castro Calls for 'Civilised Relations' with US." *BBC News*. BBC, 22 Dec. 2013. Web. 10 June 2015.

9. Mark Entwistle. "A Cheat Sheet on Issues in US-Cuba Relations." *World Affairs*. World Affairs Council of Northern California, 4 Feb. 2015. Web. 10 June 2015.

10. William M. LeoGrande and Peter Kornbluh. *Back Channel to Cuba: The Hidden History of Negotiations Between Washington and Havana*. Chapel Hill, NC: U of North Carolina P, 2014. Print. 397.

11. "2014 FIU Cuba Poll." *Cuban Research Institute*. Cuban Research Institute, 2014. Web. 10 June 2015.

INDEX

ABOUT THE
AUTHOR

Michael Capek lives in northern Kentucky with his wife and two children. He is a retired English and journalism teacher and the author of numerous books for young readers, including *The Civil Rights Movement*, *Stonehenge*, and *The D-Day Invasion of Normandy*, all published by Abdo.